13728

W9-CEP-051

# THE HINDU WORLD

## Patricia Bahree

**SILVER BURDETT COMPANY**

**Editor**
Frances Merrett
**Design**
Roland Blunk
**Picture Research**
Caroline Mitchell
**Production**
Rosemary Bishop
**Consultant**
Dr. W. Owen Cole
Senior Lecturer in Religious Studies
West Sussex Institute of Higher Education
Chichester, Sussex

First published in 1982
Macdonald & Co. (Publishers) Ltd.,
Maxwell House, Worship Street
London EC2A 2EN

© Macdonald & Co. 1982

Adapted and published in
the United States by
Silver Burdett Company,
Morristown, N.J.

**1986 Printing**

ISBN 0-382-06718-5 (Lib. Bdg.)
ISBN 0-382-06931-5

**Cover picture:** Pilgrims bathing and worshipping the sun at Varanasi.

**Endpapers:** Flower sellers at Jaipur.

**Title page:** A Hindu grandfather with his grandchild.

**Contents page:** Durga Puja celebrations.

**Library of Congress Cataloging in Publication Data**
**Bahree, Patricia.**
    The Hindu world

    (Religions of the world)
    Bibliography: p. 44.
    Includes index.
    Summary: Examines the beliefs of the hindu religion, its rites,
customs, taboos, shrines, and festivals.
    ISBN 0-382-06718-5 (lib. bdg.)

    1. Hinduism—Juvenile literature.   [1. Hinduism]   I. Title.
II. Series.
BL1203.B34   1982          294.5          83-50691
ISBN: 0-382-06931-5

# Contents

8   Hinduism and India
10  The world's oldest living faith
12  The Hindu gods—one or many?
14  Goddesses and other deities
16  The World Soul
18  A code to live by
20  Caste and village life
22  Family life in a Hindu home
24  Growing up a Hindu
26  Welcome to a Hindu wedding
28  A favourite story
30  Festival times
32  Visiting a temple
34  The sacred books
36  Mind and body
38  Places of pilgrimage
40  A rich artistic heritage
42  Useful words—a glossary
43  Special dates
44  Books for further reading
44  Places to visit
45  Index

# Hinduism and India

**Right:** These village women have come to worship in a temple in the city of Udaipur. They have covered their heads mainly as a gesture of modesty. Shoes have been left in the courtyard outside as they are never worn inside a Hindu temple. Men and women mix freely here, as they do in most Hindu temples.

## The world's third largest religion

With over 500 million followers, Hinduism ranks as the world's third largest religion. It is practised in many countries but it has a very special relationship with India. This is the land where Hinduism started centuries ago, and where over two-thirds of its followers live today.

Hinduism's most magnificent temples are in India. Many are made of stone and covered with beautiful carvings. Their tall towers stand out above the skyline of towns and cities.

The River Ganges, sacred to all Hindus, is also in India. At the ancient city of Benares the shores of the river are crowded with pilgrims who come to bathe in its holy waters.

But you need not visit the great temples or the holy Ganges to find Hinduism in India. If you walk down any street, the sights and sounds of the faith are all around you. There are pictures of gods and goddesses in almost every shop and Hindu home. You can hear the sound of temple bells and the chanting of hymns as you pass roadside shrines, and the sweet smell of incense is everywhere.

**Right:** Hinduism is very closely tied to India, where over 450 million Hindus live today. They make up about 80% of the country's population. In neighbouring Nepal, also shown in pink on this map, some 90% of the population follow the Hindu faith.

The area of India is over three and a quarter million square kilometres (about twice the size of the UK, France, West Germany and Italy combined). It is not surprising that people in different parts of this vast country live in different ways. For example, they have different languages, styles of dress and farming methods. They also practise Hinduism in different ways. Most people have the same basic beliefs, but customs and rituals can vary.

### Hindu population in Indian subcontinent

Over 80% Hindu

Less than 10% Hindu

**Right:** Roadside shrines are scattered throughout the countryside. They are often built around the base of a tree, like this one in Rajasthan.

The men carrying milk in the brass pots on their bicycles are village milkmen. The woman is performing a simple act of worship called a puja. She is sprinkling a small amount of milk over the image as an offering.

## How the word Hindu came about

Even the name 'Hindu' is tied to India—in a rather roundabout way. The river on the west of the subcontinent known today as the Indus was called the Sindhu in ancient times. The Persians who came to India had difficulty pronouncing an 's' at the beginning of a word, so they called the river the Hindu. The word was later applied to the whole land, and then to the religion practised in this part of the world. The people of India had no single word to refer to their faith. The sacred books simply speak of followers of the sacred law or *dharma*.

Most Hindus still see their faith mainly as a way of life based on the sacred laws and duties, the Hindu *dharma*.

## The faith spreads beyond India

From India, Hinduism spread to other countries. About 1000 years ago, it was carried along trade routes to lands to the east. Most of these areas were later won over by other faiths, mainly Buddhism and Islam. But Hindu influences remain in countries such as Thailand and Malaysia. In some places, like the beautiful island of Bali in Indonesia, most of the population still follow the Hindu faith.

Many Hindus also live in Europe, the USA, Canada, Africa and the West Indies. Hindu minorities in these areas tend to be the descendants of settlers from India. For example, Indian labourers came to the West Indian island of Trinidad in the late 19th century, and it is mainly their grandchildren and great-grandchildren who make up the island's large Hindu community.

Not only Hindus, but also Muslims and Sikhs from South Asia and East Africa, have settled in Britain. Some English cities have become rich multi-cultural centres. Many large towns now have at least one Hindu temple, and some have several.

In recent years growing numbers of Americans and Europeans (who have no ties with India) have turned to Hinduism. Many have become followers of Indian teachers or gurus. Although the numbers of non-Indian followers are relatively small, they do indicate a growing interest among Westerners in the teachings of the East—especially the ancient Hindu quest for inner peace and spiritual enlightenment.

# The world's oldest living faith

## No central figure or sacred book

It is difficult to pinpoint when Hinduism started or who should be given credit for its creation. It has no central figure, such as Christ in Christianity, Muhammad in Islam or the Buddha in Buddhism. Instead, it offers the teaching of many great religious thinkers who lived at different times. There is no single sacred book like the Bible or Qur'an, but many different books dating from various times and places. Hinduism is not the result of a single age, but a religion that grew up gradually, collecting together the beliefs of many groups of people.

## The roots of Hinduism

If we look for the roots of Hinduism, we have to go back several thousand years. Some roots reach back as far as the Indus valley civilization, which was thriving along the Indus river some 4000 years ago, about the same time as the great civilizations of Egypt and Mesopotamia. The Indus valley people built large cities, with neat brick houses.

Archaeologists have found many statues of a female figure in the homes of the Indus valley people. She was probably a 'Mother Goddess'. A god sitting cross-legged and surrounded by animals may be a form of the great Hindu god Shiva.

## The arrival of the Aryans

The Indus valley cities began to decline by around 1500BC, about the time a new group of people came to India. They called themselves Aryans, which means 'noble folk'. Their religious hymns remain among the most sacred writings of Hinduism. The earliest collection of hymns is the *Rig Veda*.

The Aryans came to India as nomadic tribes, moving from place to place with herds of cattle. But eventually they settled down and built their own great cities at the heart of north India, along the Ganges river.

In the early days, the sacrifice of animals to the gods was an important part of Aryan religion. In time, this ceremony lost its popularity as the feeling grew that animals should not be killed for sacrifices. Aryan ideas mixed with those of local people, some of them perhaps the descendants of the Indus valley inhabitants. A deeper level of religion developed by around 600BC. Some of the greatest religious books of Hinduism were composed at around this time. They are called the *Upanishads*.

The message of the *Upanishads* concerns the great World Soul called Brahman—which is eternal, present everywhere and embodies perfect Truth. The soul of each person is called Atman. The *Upanishads* teach that each soul is part of the World Soul. The World Soul is thus within all living things and beyond them. And all things that live are bound together by Brahman.

It was around this time that the Buddha lived and taught in India and founded the religion of Buddhism. Mahavira, on whose teaching the religion of Jainism is based, lived at about the same time.

## The spread southward

The religious ideas which developed in the north slowly spread to south India. Many of the great southern teachers emphasized a personal loving god, rather than the abstract World Soul of the *Upanishads*. They wrote hymns about the love of ordinary men and women for the great gods Shiva and Vishnu, and about the love these gods returned. Such teachings, sometimes called the *bhakti* movement, became popular throughout India. *Bhakti* means devotion. By around 400AD Hinduism had developed most of the features it has today.

## New influences

In the centuries that followed, several new faiths appeared in India. Islam became important in around 1200AD, with the arrival of Muslim conquerors who ruled much of India for several hundred years. A new religion, Sikhism, started in north India in the 16th century. It is still an important faith in the area where it was founded.

Christianity was the religion of traders who came from Europe, and of the British who came to rule much of India as a colony. But despite all these new influences, Hinduism remained the religion followed by most Indian people.

Why has Hinduism survived for so long? Part of the answer is that it is an accepting and all-embracing religion in which many local cults have found a place and become part of a great religious tradition. It allows people to seek Truth in many different ways. There is something in the Hindu faith which satisfies the greatest intellectual and also the simplest soul in their search for God.

## Some major events in the history of Hinduism

| | |
|---|---|
| **2000** | Indus valley cities thriving. |
| **1500** | Tribes of Aryans arrive in India. |
| **1200** | Sacred hymns of the *Rig Veda* in use. |
| **700** | *Upanishads* composed. |
| **500** | The Buddha teaches in India. |
| **490** | Jainism taught by Mahavira. |
| **326** | Alexander the Great invades India. |
| **250** | King Ashoka rules a vast empire. |
| **200** | Early versions of the *Ramayana* and *Mahabharata* in use. Some parts of them are much older and had been passed on orally for centuries. |
| **100** | Indian religious ideas begin to spread to Southeast Asia along trade routes. |
| **0** | Tribes from Central Asia invade India and rule territories in the Northeast. Their kings adopt Hinduism and Buddhism. |
| **300** | An early legal code, the laws of Manu, is in use. |
| **400** | The Gupta empire is at its height. The period is often called the 'golden age of Hindu culture'. Many of the features of present-day Hinduism have already come into existence. |
| **450** | Gains in mathematics and science are numerous. The decimal system is invented and used in India. Aryabhata, a Hindu astronomer, suggests that the world is round and rotates on its axis. |
| **700** | The Pallava dynasty rules most of South India. Its kings build fine temples and encourage the spread of Aryan ideas in the South. |
| **800** | The Hindu philosopher Shankara writes and teaches. |
| **900** | The Chola dynasty rules most of South India. Fine temples are built and beautiful statues cast in bronze. Strong trade ties are maintained with Southeast Asia. |
| **1000** | Northwest India invaded and parts of it ruled by Muslim overlords. Islam becomes an important religion in India and wins some converts. |
| **1100** | The Hindu philosopher Ramanuja teaches in South India. |
| **1469** | Birth of Guru Nanak, founder of the Sikh religion. |
| **1550** | Mirabai, a Rajput princess and follower of Krishna, writes beautiful devotional hymns, which are still sung in many temples. |
| **1760** | British influence growing. Christianity becomes an important religion in India and wins some converts. |
| **1900** | The Hindu philosopher and mystic Ramakrishna teaches. |
| **1930** | Mahatma Gandhi becomes an important political and religious leader. He works for Independence and stresses the end of untouchability. He encourages goodwill between Hindus, Muslims, Sikhs and Christians. |
| **1947** | India and Pakistan become independent nations. |
| **1962** | The philosopher Radhakrishnan holds the ceremonial role of President of India. Helps interpret Hinduism to the West. |
| **1970** | Vinobha Bhave, a follower of Gandhi, carries on the tradition of selfless service. Travels across India on foot encouraging landowners to give part of their land to the poor. |

# The Hindu gods—one or many?

**One god or 330 million gods**

How many gods and goddesses does Hinduism have? The figure 330 million is sometimes quoted, so is the figure one. And strange as it may seem, both are right.

At the heart of Hinduism is the belief in Brahman, the World Soul, formless and everlasting. But Hinduism also recognizes that many people need a god they can feel close to, a god they can picture in their minds and worship. The faith's many gods and goddesses fill this role. But each of them, for most Hindus, is simply one facet of the Supreme. Beyond these many gods there is really only the One.

Many Hindus apply this way of thinking not only to their religion but to all faiths. Thus, a Hindu may tell you: '*When I hear the word God, I think of Shiva or Vishnu. A Christian probably has a different mental picture. But beyond these forms, there's really only One.*' Or '*I worship all the gods—not one god in particular. But I feel God is One, whether he is Rama (the Hindu god), Allah (the word used by Muslims) or Jesus (the Christian "God made Man").*'

**Right:** Shiva is sometimes called the Lord of the Dance—*Shiva Nataraja*. This bronze statue of the dancing Shiva was made in South India in the 11th century.

Statues of Hindu gods often have a deeper meaning than first meets the eye. For instance, the dwarf on which Shiva dances represents ignorance, which he is treading under foot. The circle of flame represents the cycle of time. It has no beginning and no end.

Shiva's dancing symbolizes the eternal energy that flows through the world. It causes the pattern of day and night, the changing of the seasons and the cycle of birth and death. The energy of Shiva's dancing will eventually bring the destruction of the universe. Then, through the energy of the dance, the universe will be created again and again, through the endless cycle of time.

### Two great sects

While many Hindus offer prayers to several deities, most belong to two great sects. For one of these sects, Shiva is the main god. The other sect sees Vishnu as the centre of their faith. Vishnu is often worshipped in the form of one of his avatars or incarnations —forms he has taken on earth. Whenever evil has threatened to win over good, Vishnu has come to the aid of the human race. Most Hindus recognize ten avatars, but by far the most important are the gods Rama and Krishna.

There is also a third group that sees the goddess as being more important and powerful than any of the gods.

### Sacred images

The gods and goddesses are represented in various ways in pictures and statues. Symbols are frequently used to show their special qualities. For instance, Hindu deities usually have many arms as they have many more powers than ordinary human beings. They are often shown with an animal or bird, upon which the god or goddess rides.

**Right:** The god Vishnu is shown in this 19th-century painting sleeping on the thousand-headed serpent Shesha. The goddess Lakshmi rubs his feet.

The painting is based on a creation myth in which Vishnu has the main role. Before the creation of the universe, nothing exists except Vishnu, who sleeps on the serpent Shesha, floating in the ocean of eternity. The god Brahma emerges from a lotus that springs from his navel, and creates the world. Vishnu awakes and reigns over it. After many ages, the world is destroyed and the cycle begins again.

**Right:** The gods Shiva and Vishnu can usually be identified by what they wear and carry. **Shiva** (on the left) is often shown as a great holy man. He carries a trident, a snake and prayer beads. His clothing is the skin of a wild animal. In the centre of his head is a powerful 'third eye'. If he opens it, it will destroy everything in its path. **Vishnu** carries a lotus, a conch shell, a discus and a club. The discus is a magic weapon which he hurls at evil enemies. He wears a tall, regal crown and a jewel on his chest.

# Goddesses and other deities

## The role of the goddess

The goddess or *devi* has an important role in Hinduism. For some, she is the central deity. As such, she may be described as *shakti*, the strength and power behind all things in the universe, even the gods. In villages all over India, the *devi* is thought of as the protector of mothers and children. Her shrine is frequently visited and offerings made to her.

Among the most widely worshipped goddesses is Parvati, the wife of Shiva. At times, she can be beautiful and gentle. At other times she takes the form of the warrior goddess, Durga, who rides on the back of a lion and slays the evil buffalo demon. Sometimes she is Kali—ugly and terrifying, wearing a garland of human skulls, the bringer of disease, strife and war.

Vishnu's wife is Lakshmi, the goddess of good luck and good fortune. She is often shown seated on a lotus blossom with elephants spraying water over her.

## The minor gods

Brahma was once an important god, but his popularity has declined over the centuries. Still, he is often found among the many figures carved on a temple wall. He usually has four faces, and his vehicle is a swan. The wife of Brahma is the beautiful goddess Saraswati, patron of art, music and literature. Her vehicle is also a swan and she carries a *vina* (musical instrument) and a book.

Hanuman, the monkey god, is popular in cities and villages all over India. When Sita, wife of the god Rama, was kidnapped by an evil demon, Hanuman and his army of monkeys came to the rescue and helped Rama save her. In homage to Hanuman, monkeys are rarely harmed in India.

One of the most cheerful of Hindu deities is Ganesh, the elephant-headed god. His vehicle is a rat, although it is hard to imagine him riding on it. Ganesh is shown as a prosperous pot-bellied god, who often carries a bowl of sweets. He is the Lord of Obstacles and will remove any hurdles his worshippers may face. His help is often sought at the start of any important job. The first prayers in a *puja* (short ritual, form of worship) may be offered to him. He is interested in books and is the Lord of Grammarians. Many books printed in India have a small picture of him on the title page or the phrase '*Shri Ganesha Namah*' (reverence to Lord Ganesh).

**Right:** The World Soul, Brahman, has no shape or form. It is present everywhere, eternally. No picture of it could ever be made.

For most Hindus the gods and goddesses are different ways of picturing the divine. A few of them are shown here.

In the top row three different forms of the same goddess are shown (from left to right). As **Parvati** she is kind and gentle. She holds her son, the elephant-headed god **Ganesh**. As **Durga**, the warrior-goddess, she rides a lion. As **Kali** she wears a necklace of skulls and is the bringer of war and disease.

The monkey god **Hanuman** is shown next, leaping through the sky carrying a mountain. On it grows four special herbs, which will cure the wounded army of the god Rama.

**Indra** is on the far left of the second row. He rides on an elephant and is both a war god and weather god. It is Indra who brings storms and thunder. Next comes **Surya**, the sun god, who drives his flaming chariot across the sky each day, then **Chandra**, the moon god, who drives his silvery chariot across the heavens at night.

**Lakshmi** (shown on the far left of the bottom row) is the goddess of good fortune. She is the wife of Vishnu and carries the conch shell and lotus, which are also his emblems.

Next comes the beautiful **Saraswati**, goddess of wisdom and learning, and then her husband, the four-headed god **Brahma**, who carries a book of the *Vedas* as well as an alms bowl and sceptre. Last is **Agni**, the fire god. Agni is present wherever there is fire.

Parvati

Ganesh

Indra

Lakshmi

# The World Soul

### Recurring questions

People have always asked questions about the meaning of life such as why is there so much suffering in the world? Will good people one day be rewarded and evil-doers punished? Why do people die—and what happens after death?

Hinduism's basic beliefs offer answers to these questions, and many others. Hindus are not bound to these teachings, however. A person may accept some of the teachings and not others, and still remain a Hindu. (For the views of some young Hindus, see page 18.) However, most Hindus share many of these basic beliefs.

### The cycle of birth and death

Perhaps the most important teaching of Hinduism is that the soul is born many times on earth. The body may grow old and die, but the soul lives on, reborn in another human form or in some other living thing.

The body that the soul lives in during the next life depends on one's actions in this life. If one does good deeds, he or she will be reborn at a higher level. But if the bad outweighs the good, the soul will be reborn in a lower form. This chain of cause and effect is called the law of *karma* (deeds), and it is one's deeds that determine the conditions of one's next life.

**Sunrise on the holy River Ganges**

While life on earth has many good aspects, the ultimate aim is to break the cycle of birth and death—to gain release or *moksha*, never to be born again. This happens when the individual soul, or *Atman*, achieves total oneness with the World Soul, Brahman. It is merged with Brahman in an eternal state of perfect knowledge and perfect bliss.

## Paths to salvation

Hinduism offers several paths to this ultimate goal. One path is spiritual knowledge. Insight is gained by meditation and yoga. Through many years of effort, the person scales greater and greater spiritual heights, until enlightenment is reached.

Another important path is that of devotion, of loving God totally with one's whole heart. A third is the path of works, which means selflessly serving one's fellow human beings and working for the good of society.

The majority of Hindus are more concerned with working hard and living a good and happy life than seeking *moksha* (release). It must be remembered that Hinduism is a faith of many levels. Only a very few people put everyday life behind them, devoting their time only to spiritual matters and attempting to break the cycle of birth and death.

# A code to live by

### The caste system

Tied to the idea of rebirth is that of caste—the basis for social divisions in Hinduism. Each Hindu is born into a caste group. The castes are ranked one above the other. Whether one is born into a high or low caste depends on the deeds of one's previous life.

Hinduism divides society into four large classes, called the four *varnas*. At the top are the Brahmins, who are considered the purest, and perform all religious ceremonies. Next come the Kshatriyas, who were traditionally rulers and warriors. The third group are the Vaishyas, traders and craft workers. Fourth are the Shudras, the ordinary workers. At the bottom is a fifth group, who are outside the caste system. Traditionally this group was considered polluted and untouchable and did all the dirtiest jobs. Today, classing people as untouchable has been officially outlawed but attitudes sometimes change slowly.

The varna divisions are not the whole story, however. There are, in fact, hundreds of small caste groups in India. These are often called *jati*. A person's jati may determine the exact job a person has and influence his or her life in many important

---

### Young Hindus talk about their beliefs

What do younger Hindus think about concepts such as karma and caste? Here are a few answers from teenage Hindus living in India today.

**What do you consider the most important belief of Hinduism?**
**Neela:** I consider rebirth the most important belief—that the soul is immortal. The body perishes but the soul simply changes form.
**Deepaka:** The most important aspect of Hinduism is being truthful to yourself. Hinduism may have many beliefs, but if you aren't truthful to yourself, you can't follow any of them.
**Kishan:** Hinduism teaches tolerance towards all religions. It teaches you to serve mankind, to do your duty and to follow your conscience.

**Do you feel that people who do evil are punished? If so, how and when?**
**Kishan:** One of the most important beliefs in Hinduism is the karma theory—that a person is rewarded according to the deeds he or she does. But I think people are punished in this world, either by the laws of society or by mental suffering.
**Deepaka:** Yes, I feel evil deeds are punished—revenge follows or you suffer heavy losses. It may come in this life or the next.

**Do you think the law of karma explains the fact that some people are poor and hungry while others have more money than they can spend?**
**Deepaka:** No. Usually it's the result of economic circumstances. About 80% of the people in India are poor. I don't think that means that 80% have done evil deeds.
**Kishan:** No, I don't. Some people are poor and hungry in India because the resources simply don't meet the demand. Some are rich because they saw an opportunity—and they took it.

**Do you believe in untouchability? And do you think the caste system can survive in the modern world?**
**Neela:** No, I don't believe in untouchability. The caste system was originally based on the occupation of each person. But in the modern world it's not applicable or practical.
**Savita:** I personally don't believe in untouchability. But it's still there in most parts of India. Even in modern homes untouchable sweepers come to do the cleaning. No one will touch them. Untouchability shouldn't survive, but it has survived and it will survive. I don't see any power that can remove it from India.
**Deepaka:** No, I don't believe in untouchability. The caste system is just different groups of people. Nobody asks your caste before becoming your friend.

**Right:** An elderly man reads in a peaceful spot. It is likely that he has left the stage of the householder behind him, and turned to religious things. However, he probably won't actually leave his home and become a wandering sanyasin. He has adapted the third and fourth stages of Hindu life to fit his own circumstances.

**Right:** The gap between rich and poor is shown very clearly here. The lifestyles of these Bombay fisherwomen and those of people living in the luxury of high-rise blocks are very different.

Some Hindus believe that material wealth is directly linked with good actions in a previous life. But many Hindus say that poverty is the result of economic circumstances which can be changed.

ways (see pages 20–21). Each of the small caste groups belongs to one of the five great divisions. And all of society is arranged like a gigantic ladder.

## The four stages of life

Hinduism also offers a plan for living one's life. Ideally, each person should pass through four stages, or *ashramas*: that of student, householder, 'forest dweller' and wandering holy man (*sanyasin*). Some Hindus, but not many, pass through the four stages but most spend much of their adult lives as householders. Elderly people may adapt the third stage and spend much of their time in prayer and meditation while living in a son's home.

## Following one's dharma

An important concept of Hinduism that ties together other beliefs is that of *dharma*— which can be translated as sacred law. Following the sacred law means doing good and not evil. It also means doing what is right for you, based on the caste group you were born into and the stage of life you have reached.

# Caste and village life

### A position in life

Caste plays an important role in the life of most Hindus. This is especially true in the villages of India where 75% of the population lives. If you were a Hindu living in a village, here are some ways caste might influence your life.

Your caste group would probably determine the job you had. Most castes are linked with a traditional occupation which is passed on from father to son. If your father was a carpenter, he would teach you his trade.

Your caste group would also influence whom you married. Most marriages in India are arranged by parents. Your parents would choose someone from the same caste group, but probably from a different village.

Your economic status would be partly influenced by your caste. If you were from one of the higher castes, the chances are you would be one of the more prosperous people in the village. If you were from one of the lower castes, you would probably be poorer and work for one of the upper castes. This is not always the case, but it is the general rule.

### Caste and ritual purity

Your caste would also determine whom you would share food with. Behind the ranking system is the idea of ritual purity. The higher you are on the caste ladder, the greater your purity is. Many Hindus are reluctant to accept food from someone of a lower caste group for this reason.

Ritual purity is also behind the idea of untouchability. According to traditional thinking, people who do certain kinds of work are impure. These include, for instance, people who clean the streets for the rest of the community. Other members of the village avoid contact with the untouchables. If they do accidentally touch them, they bathe and perform rituals to make themselves pure again. The great Indian leader Mahatma Gandhi said untouchability was a blot on Hinduism and worked to remove it. He called the untouchables *Harijans* (children of God). Many Hindus agree with his thinking. Many people from the untouchable castes are now more educated and demand their rights as equal citizens.

Some Hindus are against untouchability but are in favour of the caste system. They point out that the caste system has kept villages running smoothly by providing a place and role for everyone. It has enabled many different groups to enter the fold of Hinduism, since they could keep a separate identity and still be part of the whole. Caste has also provided a sort of welfare system at the village level. If people are in need, they can turn to their caste for help. Most caste groups in a village have a caste council which finds ways to help needy members, such as widows or orphans. Perhaps most important, caste has kept village life stable, even while empires rose and fell.

**Right:** This woman is from the basketmakers' caste and the man behind her is the village carpenter. The traditional caste system covered all the jobs that needed to be done in a village.

Basketmakers made baskets for the whole village, and the carpenter provided his service for the entire community. All jobs were passed down through the family, which helped to make a stable society.

**Right:** The entire family of the village potter may help in the work. Here the pots are being fired, with cakes of cow dung used as fuel. Though making pots of so many shapes and sizes takes skill, the potter is low in the caste ranking system.

**Right:** A city barber performs his job in the open air. Barbers form a separate caste. They teach their trade to their sons, who will also be barbers.

Barbers are rated fairly low on the caste scale. Yet they often have close ties with the higher caste families they serve. In a village, it may be the barber who acts as a go-between to help arrange marriages.

# Family life in a Hindu home

## Families large and small

For many Hindus, family life means being part of a large family with grandparents, parents, aunts, uncles and children all living under one roof. However, not all Hindus live in large family groups. In cities, families often consist of parents and children only. Sometimes a grandparent, a maiden aunt or a cousin from a village joins the family.

## Prayers in the home

Prayer is a part of the daily routine in most Hindu households. Almost every Hindu home has a family shrine. It may have a statue of one or several gods or goddesses, or pictures, perhaps of Krishna and Rama.

In the early morning, a Hindu home will be full of the sounds of bathing and praying. Most Hindus do not eat breakfast until they have bathed and said their prayers.

The prayers may take the form of a short ritual called a *puja*, performed at the family shrine. Incense is lit and flowers, fruit or a coconut are placed in front of the image as an offering. Water may be sprinkled on the image and an oil lamp or candle lit in front of it. Prayers are offered in front of the image

**Right:** A village woman performs a puja in front of a shrine she has made outside her home. Most Hindus see praying as part of everyday life and are not embarrassed about it. The man in the background reads a newspaper. Both people are absorbed in the activities that make up their 'morning routine'.

as part of the puja ceremony.

Instead of performing a puja, some people sit in a peaceful place and read from the holy books. Others may recite the names of gods, counting them off on prayer beads. Many Hindus also begin the day with meditation or yoga. Most Hindus are not in the least embarrassed about praying. In a city household, if there is an early morning phone call, the caller may be told that the mother or father will come to the phone as soon as they have finished their prayers.

In many Hindu homes, some or all family members may bathe again in the evening and perform a short puja, or offer prayers to mark the end of another day.

## Respect for elders

Respect for elders is an important part of Hindu family values. In a large family, important decisions will usually be made jointly by older family members.

One important role for parents is choosing marriage partners for their sons and daughters. Most Hindu teenagers are happy to leave the choice of a partner to their elders, trusting that with their greater experience they will make a good choice. (For a description of the marriage ceremony, see pages 26–27.)

The bride usually goes to live in the groom's home. She will come from a similar family background, so the adjustment to married life should not be difficult.

Marriage is considered a religious duty by many Hindus. Children (especially a son) are important to continue the family line and perform rites for family members who are no longer living.

## Some family customs

Respect for elders is also shown in many small ways. For instance, when a Hindu boy who has been studying in a different town comes home for the holidays, he will greet his parents first by touching their feet to show respect and then by embracing them.

At home, a woman, no matter how old she is, will usually cover her head when her husband's father enters the room. If she is wearing a *sari* (traditional woman's dress) she will pull the long, flowing end over her head. If she is wearing a *shalwar-kameeze* (a long, loose shirt and trousers) she will cover her head with a scarf called a *dupatta* that is worn at the neck.

If a man smokes, he will not smoke in front of his father, and often not in front of an uncle or elder brother.

In the family life of Hindus, the tie between children and grandparents may be especially strong, since grandparents often look after young children. The 'old people's homes' of Europe and America are shocking places in the eyes of many Hindus. Few Hindus would want to break family ties by sending a respected parent or grandparent to live in an institution.

**Right:** A young girl performs a puja at a family shrine. Pictures and statues of deities have been placed on the household altar. During the puja, candles and incense are lit and prayers offered. Members of the family may pray here alone or together.

**Right:** Hindu families gather at a temple in England. There are close ties between the generations in most Hindu families and very often young and old share family activities.

The children learn about their religion from their parents, aunts, uncles and grandparents. Here the children are helping to perform the *arti* ceremony. In this simple rite an oil lamp is held before the image and moved in front of it in a circular pattern to form a circle of light.

23

# Growing up a Hindu

**Right:** Most Hindus have a horoscope cast shortly after they are born. The horoscope shows the position of planets and stars at the moment of birth. Many Hindus believe that future events can be foretold from a horoscope.

Some Hindu priests and other people specialize in casting and reading horoscopes. This man has set up a roadside stall to tell people what is in store for them, on the basis of their horoscope.

## Ceremonies for different stages of life

Every faith has its rites of passage, to mark important steps in life. Hinduism has lots of ceremonies and many of them take place in childhood. The ceremonies are not exactly the same for all Hindus, as people of different castes and in different parts of India have different customs.

## When a baby is born

The arrival of a baby in a Hindu home is a big occasion. Preparations are likely to include special ceremonies performed before the baby is born for the welfare of the mother and child. Most Hindu families in India and many abroad have a family priest. He will be a Brahmin, and will usually come to the family's home to perform various rites.

When the baby is born, it is welcomed into the world with a short ceremony. The priest or one of the family whispers special prayers into the baby's ear and a mixture of honey and *ghee* (similar to melted butter) is placed on its tongue. The house may be decorated with strings of leaves from special trees to mark the happy event.

## Naming the baby

The naming ceremony usually takes place ten days after the baby is born. The baby's horoscope is cast at the same time, based on the exact minute the baby was born. The priest often chooses the letter that the name will start with, based on the horoscope. If it is an 'A', a boy might be called *Anand*

**Right:** A boy receives the 'sacred thread'. The 'sacred thread' ceremony is an elaborate and impressive rite. Hindu men often look back on this day as the most exciting and memorable in their childhood.

The rite is performed before a fire lit in a special vessel. There are also offerings of fruit and other food.

The older men in the picture are priests and family members. They all wear the 'sacred thread'. The vertical marks on their foreheads indicate that they are followers of the god Vishnu.

**Right:** Hindu girls in England perform a special 'stick dance' for the festival of Navratri.

Although these girls are growing up far away from India, they will have learned this traditional Indian dance from their mothers and will probably teach it to their daughters too.

(which means happy) or a girl *Asha* (which means hope). If the letter is an 'R', a boy might be called *Ram* (the name of a god) or a girl *Rani* (which means princess). Hindu names are usually chosen because they have a special meaning.

### 'Sacred thread' ceremony

By far the most important ceremony of childhood is the initiation or 'sacred thread' ceremony. This rite is for boys, and only for those boys of the top three classes—Brahmins, Kshatriyas and Vaishyas. It usually takes place between the ages of eight and eleven. It is an elaborate ceremony during which a Brahmin priest hangs a long loop of thread, made of several strands twisted together, over the boy's left shoulder and under his right arm. The sacred thread is worn from that day onward.

This ceremony is thought of as a second birth and those who wear the sacred thread are called the 'twice born'. After this ceremony the boy begins to learn more of the sacred writings and rituals of his religion, some of which are taught only to the 'twice born'.

### Learning about the faith

One of the most important parts of religious education for children is learning values, customs and duties from other members of the family. Grandparents may play a special role in passing on the traditions by telling children bedtime stories about the gods and goddesses and teaching them religious songs.

When the children are old enough, the Brahmin priest may visit their home to teach them more about their faith. This may include lessons in Sanskrit, the ancient language in which many of the sacred books are written.

### Hinduism's broad view

In modern India most schools do not have lessons on Hinduism, but children study morals and ethics in which the beliefs of various religions are discussed. Plays and other events may reflect the religions represented in the school. There may be a display or event on the birthday of Guru Nanak, founder of the Sikh faith; a play about Rama and Sita for the Hindu holiday of Dussehra and a special pageant for Christmas.

25

# Welcome to a Hindu wedding

### Jasmine, roses and marigolds

The time is 11 pm, yes, eleven o'clock at night! The place is a garden somewhere in India. A Brahmin priest sits under a canopy (tent-like roof), which has been decorated with chains of jasmine flowers, roses and marigolds. A crowd gathers round.

A young woman enters with her female relatives and friends. She's wearing a bright red sari and her jewellery glistens in the lamplight. A young man approaches from the opposite direction, with the male members of his family. His face is covered by a veil made of strings of flowers. When they meet in front of the priest, the man places a garland of flowers around the neck of the woman, and she places one around his neck. What's happening? A Hindu marriage ceremony has just begun.

### Before the sacred fire

Hindu weddings differ from place to place, but usually follow a similar pattern. The ceremony is often held in the courtyard of the bride's house or in a nearby square or even a blocked-off street, but not in a temple.

The time is set by the priest after he has studied the stars and planets to determine the most auspicious moment. It could be 4 am or 2 pm. The groom usually arrives for the wedding on horseback like a prince, preceded by a brass band and surrounded by friends and relatives.

The ceremony itself is performed before a fire lit in a special metal vessel. The priest recites hymns from the sacred texts in Sanskrit and the bride and groom pour small offerings of rice and *ghee* (clarified butter) into the flames. The most important part of the ceremony comes when a knot is tied between the bride's sari and the groom's *kurta* (long shirt) and the couple walk around the fire together seven times.

### Choosing a marriage partner

At a Hindu wedding the bride and groom may be meeting for the first time. Most Hindu marriages are arranged by the parents (see page 22).

The idea behind arranged marriages is that love comes gradually, after marriage and not before. The love often seen in Hindu households would tend to prove the point.

**Right:** The bride prepares for her wedding. This Hindu marriage is taking place in England. The bride has probably spent several hours in preparation, with the help of her mother, sisters and women friends.

Several days before a marriage, the bride's hands and feet may be decorated using a special plant called *mehndi*. Its leaves are crushed to make a paste. Patterns are drawn on the skin with the paste and when it is washed away the skin beneath is dyed red. The decoration lasts for several weeks.

The special facial make-up that this bride is wearing is applied just before the marriage ceremony. It washes off easily after the wedding. Special jewellery is often worn by the bride, like the gold chain decorating this bride's hair.

**Right:** A bride with sisters and friends. The bride, in the red sari, wears special make-up which has been applied just before the wedding. The red dot that many Hindu women wear in the centre of the forehead is purely decorative and can be worn by married and unmarried women. A married woman can also put red powder in the parting of her hair (as the woman in the yellow sari has done).

There are several other signs to show that a woman is married. In some Hindu communities, special toe rings are worn as well as the more common wedding ring on the finger. A necklace called a *mangalsutra* is also worn only by married women.

**Right:** A night-time wedding in New Delhi. The ceremony is taking place in the garden of the bride's home, which has been decorated with strings of flowers. The priest is on the right. The bride and groom sit in front of the sacred fire.

Various kinds of food are offered in the ceremony. The groom's parents, on the left, hold the bride's hand as part of the ceremony. A Hindu wedding ceremony like this takes several hours to perform.

27

# A favourite story

## Krishna, hero of many stories

Hinduism offers a rich and almost endless array of stories. The hero of many of the best loved and most often told tales is Krishna, the eighth avatar of Vishnu. Krishna (whose name literally means 'the dark one') is usually shown with dark blue skin. He wears a peacock feather in his hair and carries a flute, on which he plays enchanting tunes. Here are some stories about this well-loved god.

Krishna was born of royal blood, but did not grow up enjoying the luxuries of palace life. Shortly after his birth, he was carried off to the countryside to the home of the cowherds Nanda and Yashoda. Their baby, a daughter born at the same time as Krishna, was left in his place. The switch was made because the wicked King Kansa had been warned that a baby born in the palace would one day take over his kingdom.

As soon as he heard that a child had arrived, he rushed to the mother's room, snatched the baby girl left in Krishna's place, threw the small sweet infant against the hard stone floor and crushed her. A goddess sprang from the body of the dead baby and told King Kansa that his doom was sealed. Krishna was still alive and safe in a distant corner of the kingdom and one day would return to bring good and righteous rule to the land.

Krishna grew up enjoying the simple pleasures of country life—romping with his friends in the forest, making wreaths of leaves and garlands of wild flowers, and playing his flute. He was a mischievous child, however. The village women made butter from the milk they got from their cows. When they weren't looking, Krishna stole their butter and ate it.

His mother, Yashoda, loved him so much she rarely scolded him. However, one day, the other children came running to her. 'Krishna,' they told her, 'has been eating dirt.' Fearing for his health, she ordered Krishna to open his mouth. He did. And then she saw the entire universe—the sky, the earth, the sun, the moon and the stars—and realized her son was God and that all the world was contained within him. Yashoda fainted. When she awoke, she had forgotten what she saw. She took Krishna on her lap, kissed him, and held him.

## Meeting the serpent

When he was still a boy, Krishna overcame many demons who threatened him or the other cowherds. One of these demons was a terrible serpent who made his home in a river near the place where the cowherds lived. The serpent's fiery breath had scorched the leaves of the trees and bushes near the stream. Birds that flew through its path were burnt to a cinder.

One day Krishna went to the place where the serpent lived. He summoned the great snake by slapping the foaming water with

**Right:** Today many Hindu children read the great stories of their faith in comic books. One of the most popular is the story of the *Mahabharata*, a scene from which is shown here.

The first picture shows the god Krishna and the warrior Arjuna. In the next two pictures Krishna takes the form of Arjuna's charioteer. He encourages the warrior and tells him why he must fight hard in the battle.

BUT AS THE ZERO HOUR APPROACHED, ARJUNA WAS OVERCOME WITH EMOTION.

OH KRISHNA! THESE ARE MEN OF MY OWN BLOOD! I HAVE NO WISH TO KILL THEM.

TAKE HEART, ARJUNA! YOU CAN'T RUN AWAY NOW.

**Right:** As a child Krishna saved his friends from many dangers. In this 18th-century painting, he swallows a forest fire which threatens to kill them. The artist's love for the cows that the boys are tending is clear from the beautiful way he's drawn them.

Cows have a very special place in Hinduism. They may not be killed and beef is never eaten by Hindus. This is partly because all life is sacred to Hindus. They feel cows should be protected because they produce the milk and cheese which help young and old, rich and poor to keep healthy.

his hand. When the many-headed serpent appeared, Krishna leapt on its billowing snake hoods and began to dance. He danced faster and faster, forcing the great snake down beneath the waves. The snake's wives begged Krishna to spare the serpent's life. The serpent itself told Krishna: 'I have only acted according to my nature. As You created me, so I have behaved.' Krishna took pity on the serpent and did not kill it, but sent it to live in the depths of the ocean where it could not harm anyone.

Krishna grew up to be a handsome young man who stole the hearts of all the village women. He eventually returned to the palace where he was born, killed the wicked Kansa and ruled as a wise king.

The Krishna stories can be interpreted in many different ways. They show that there are many ways to love God—as a mother loves a son, as a child loves his friends, as a woman loves a man, or as a citizen loves a wise and just ruler. The stories also show that Krishna loves those who turn to him and will guide them and protect them from the evils of the world.

# Festival times

### The Hindu Calendar

Hinduism has many holidays. Some are celebrated by most Hindus, and others only among certain communities or in special places. Here are details of some holidays. (The calendar of festivals at the back of this book describes a few more.)

Most of the Hindu holidays are based on the Hindu calendar, developed in ancient India. It has twelve months, worked out according to the phases of the moon. Dussehra falls in the month of Asvina on the Hindu calendar, which is usually October on the Gregorian calendar used in the West.

### Dussehra, triumph of good over evil

Dussehra is celebrated in most parts of India and by Hindu communities all over the world, although various groups mark the holiday in different ways. Celebrations usually last for ten days. In northern India, barley is planted in small dishes on the first day. By the tenth day the young shoots look like those in the fields. The plants have a special place on the family shrine.

As well as being tied to the farming cycle, Dussehra celebrates the triumph of good over evil. In eastern India, the victory of the goddess Durga over the Buffalo Demon is the main focus of the holiday. In other parts of India, the holiday marks the victory of the god Rama (an avatar of Vishnu) over the demon king Ravana. Though he was a prince, Rama had been banished from his kingdom and forced to live in the forest. There his beautiful wife Sita was captured and carried off by the evil Ravana. But Rama defeated the demon with the help of Hanuman and his monkey army.

The story of Rama is told in the sacred book the *Ramayana*. At the time of Dussehra the story is acted out in cities and villages. The play is called the Rama Lila. On the tenth night the actor playing Rama fires a flaming arrow into a giant paper statue of the demon Ravana, which has been filled with firecrackers. Ravana is destroyed with a bang! (See the illustration on page 41.)

### The festival of lights

Divali falls in the Hindu month of Karttika (October-November). Its name comes from the Sanskrit word *dipavali*, which means a row of lights. Divali marks the return of Rama to his kingdom to become the rightful king. People light rows of small oil lamps or candles along windows and balconies to welcome Rama home.

Lakshmi, the goddess of wealth, is also worshipped on Divali. In most parts of India, Divali marks the new year. Businesses open new account books at this time. A ceremony called the Lakshmi puja is performed to bring good fortune in the coming year. An oil lamp is left burning in most homes all night to welcome the goddess.

Divali is also a time when people wear new clothes, visit friends and exchange sweets.

### Holi and other holidays

One holiday that's great fun is Holi, which falls at the start of India's hot season in February-March. A bonfire is lit on the eve of Holi. The next morning all barriers of caste and rank are forgotten, as people throw coloured water and bright powders at each other. Students chase their teachers down the street and workers spray their bosses. In the afternoon, people go home for a bath. The evening is a time for visiting and exchanging sweets. People embrace each other and offer good wishes.

**Left:** These children have been 'playing Holi' (throwing brightly coloured powders to mark the holiday). After they clean up they will visit friends and exchange sweets with them.

30

**Right:** Durga Puja celebrations. Large statues of the goddess Durga slaying the buffalo demon are specially made for the holiday. They are the focus of worship in neighbourhood shrines. At the close of celebrations, the images (often made of paper maché) are carried in a procession to the nearest large area of water and immersed there.

Durga carries many weapons which the gods gave her to help her slay the demon. In this picture, the buffalo demon (barely visible) is lying at her feet.

**Right:** Hindu businessmen living in London gather together to perform a Divali puja, with their account books in front of them. Divali is the time when old account books are closed and new ones opened. The puja is performed partly to bring prosperity in the coming year.

The red mark on the forehead is called a *tilak*. It is made from a red powder and applied by a priest, a member of the family or a friend when a puja is performed.

# Visiting a temple

**Right:** An artist's impression of the Brahmeshvara temple at Bhubaneshwar, in the state of Orissa, built in the 9th century. The main parts are: a pillared hallway, small shrine room and tall tower. A wall surrounds the temple with four small shrines situated at the corners.

Inside the main shrine the god Shiva is represented in the form of the linga. The *linga* is generally considered to be a symbol of the masculine forces of the universe, emphasizing Shiva's powers of creation.

A statue of Shiva's vehicle (the bull) Nandi stands in the hallway directly in front of the linga.

## Large and small, old and new

Hindu temples come in many varieties. A village shrine in India may be a mud or thatch shelter with a simple image inside. In Britain, Hindu communities have often converted houses or recreation halls into temples. However, most large temples in India are built according to an age-old design.

## A typical temple plan

Most temples are surrounded by walls, which separate the sanctified space of the temple from the everyday world outside. To enter the temple, you must first pass through a gateway, which can be simple or a towering, ornately carved structure.

Inside the wall, there may be several small shrines as well as the main temple. There may also be a tank, a well or a tap where worshippers can bathe so that they enter the temple in a pure state.

There is usually a bell at the entrance of the main temple, which you ring as you enter. Leading to the heart of the temple are several pillared hallways containing statues of various gods and goddesses. The main image is usually at the very back of the temple in a small, dark chamber lit with oil lamps. Sometimes a small passage is left so that worshippers can walk around the image as a sign of reverence.

Most temples have a tall tower rising above the spot where the main image stands. The tower and sides of the temple may be carved with statues of gods and goddesses, men and women, and plants and animals.

## Worship in the temple

Hindus may visit a temple alone or in small family groups. Men, women and children all worship together, but there is no set congregational service like that held at a Christian church on Sunday or a Muslim mosque on Friday. In fact, there is no obligation for believers to visit a temple at all, although most Hindus do.

Worship in a temple consists mainly of performing a puja, similar to that held in the home. It varies somewhat from place to place, but generally gifts such as sweets and flowers are presented to the god or goddess. A priest (who sits near the main image) then makes a mark on the worshipper's forehead with red powder.

Silent prayers are offered for a few minutes. Then most of the sweets which have been placed before the image are returned to the worshipper, who eats a small part and distributes the rest among the poor, keeping some to take home to other members of the family.

Many people visit a temple on their way to work in the morning and place a flower in front of the image of the god or goddess and pause for a few minutes to pray, before going on their way.

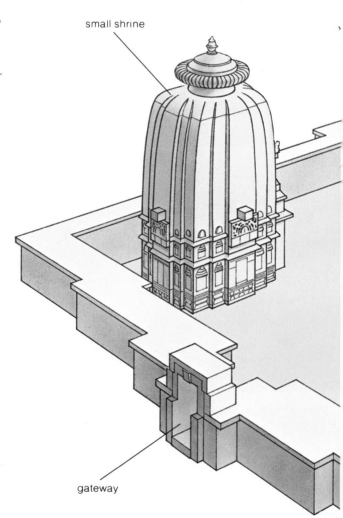

small shrine

gateway

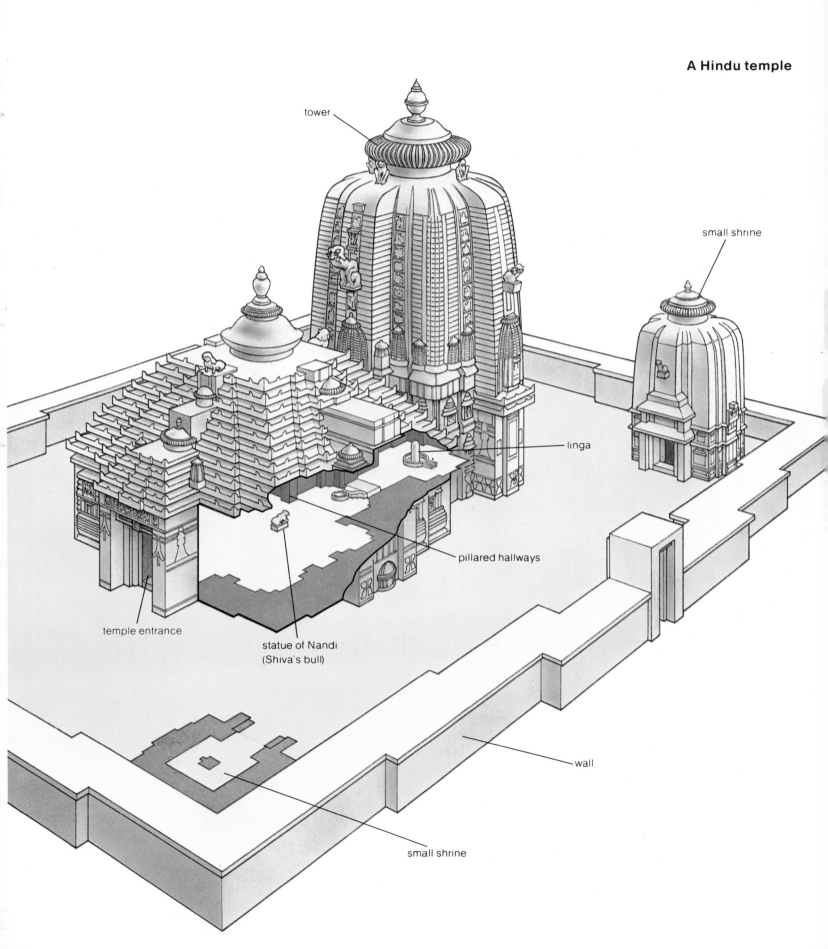

A Hindu temple

tower

small shrine

linga

pillared hallways

temple entrance

statue of Nandi
(Shiva's bull)

wall

small shrine

33

# The sacred books

**The *Vedas* and *Upanishads***

Hinduism's sacred books are many and varied. The oldest are the four *Vedas*, of which the earliest and most sacred is the *Rig Veda* (a collection of 1028 hymns). Most of the hymns of the *Rig Veda* were in use by around 1000BC. The *Sama, Yajur,* and *Atharva Vedas* came into use later and parts of them are based on the *Rig Veda*. The *Vedas* are in Sanskrit, the language of ancient India. They were passed on orally for hundreds of years before they were written down.

The *Upanishads* (the sessions) date from around 600BC, and are among Hinduism's most important scriptures. They contain the wisdom that was passed on in sessions between religious teachers and their students. The *Upanishads* are concerned with the World Soul, called Brahman, and teach that the soul of every living thing (the Self) is Brahman. When the individual soul (Atman) achieves total oneness with the World Soul (Brahman), a person achieves *moksha*, and gains release from the cycle of birth and death.

**Epic poems and devotional hymns**

Hinduism's great epic poems, the *Mahabharata* and *Ramayana*, were written in the period between 300BC and 300AD. The *Mahabharata* tells the story of a great civil war between two branches of the ruling family. It is probably the longest poem in the world, with over 90,000 stanzas. One of the most important parts of the *Mahabharata* is a section called the *Bhagavad Gita*, which means 'The Song of God'. In it Lord Krishna makes a moving and beautiful speech to the warrior Arjuna, restating many of the basic beliefs of the faith and stressing the virtue of selfless service.

The *Ramayana* is the story of Rama, the avatar of Vishnu, his banishment to the forest, the rescue of his wife Sita from the demon king Ravana and his eventual return home to become a wise and just king.

Among Hinduism's most popular literature are collections of devotional hymns. These were written by various poets in local languages as well as Sanskrit. The central theme is the worshipper's love of God, whether Krishna or Shiva.

The *Puranas* (which means 'ancient stories') are collections of myths which were compiled over hundreds of years. The oldest parts may date back as far as 400BC, while newer sections may be dated from 1000AD.

**Right:** Worshippers gather to hear a priest read from one of the holy books at the Jagdish Temple in Udaipur. The reading is taking place among the beautifully carved stone pillars in the hallway leading to the main shrine. The *Bhagavad Gita* is a favourite book for such occasions.

**Right:** This verse from the *Upanishads* is written in Sanskrit, the language of ancient India. The script is written from left to right, like English. Most of Hinduism's ancient sacred books are written in Sanskrit. An English translation of this verse is shown beneath it.

ॐ　असतो मा सद्गमय।
तमसो मा ज्योतिर्गमय।
मृत्योर्मास्मृतं गमय ॥

*From delusion lead me to Truth.*
*From darkness lead me to Light.*
*From death lead me to immortality.*

**Brihad-Aranyaka Upanishad 1, 3, 28**

Here are some excerpts from the *Upanishads* which have inspired Hindus and influenced writers, philosophers, poets and artists all over the world.

*He who has not right understanding and whose mind is never steady is not the ruler of his life, like a bad driver with wild horses. But he who has right understanding and whose mind is ever steady is the ruler of his life, like a good driver with well-trained horses. He who has not right understanding is careless and never pure, reaches not the End of the journey; but wanders from death to death. But he who has understanding, is careful and ever pure, reaches the End of the journey, from which he never returns. . . .*

**Katha Upanishad**

*The Atman is beyond sound and form, without touch and taste and perfume. It is eternal, unchangeable and without beginning or end: indeed above reasoning. When consciousness of the Atman manifests itself, man becomes free from the jaws of death. . . .*

**Katha Upanishad**

*Words cannot describe the joy of the soul whose impurities are cleansed in deep contemplation—who is one with his Atman, his own Spirit. Only those who feel this joy know what it is.*

*Even as water becomes one with water, fire with fire, and air with air, so the mind becomes one with the Infinite Mind and thus attains final freedom.*

**Maitri Upanishad**

*There is a Spirit which is pure and which is beyond old age and death; and beyond hunger and thirst and sorrow. This is Atman, the Spirit in man. All the desires of this Spirit are Truth. It is this Spirit that we must find and know: Man must find his own Soul. He who has found and knows his Soul has found all the worlds, has achieved all his desires.*

**Chandogya Upanishad**

All these excerpts are taken from *The Upanishads*, translated by Juan Mascaro (Penguin Classics, 1965) from pp. 60–61; 103; 121; 127. Copyright © Juan Mascaro, 1965. Reprinted by permission of Penguin Books Ltd.

# Mind and body

## Yoga—control of mind and body

Several years ago a number of Hindu holy men were invited to a research clinic in New Delhi, India, to take part in scientific experiments. They were experts at yoga—a series of exercises aimed at controlling the mind and body. A person who practises yoga is called a *yogi* (male) or *yogini* (female). The scientists wanted to find out if these yogis had gained any special powers. The experiments showed that, indeed, they had. The yogis could control their breathing and live for a longer time on a smaller amount of air than an ordinary person. They were also able to control the rhythm of their heartbeat and withstand extremes of hot and cold with no physical reaction.

## Salvation, the yogi's goal

The exercises that yogis practise date back to the early history of Hinduism. The traditional religious goal of the yogi was salvation, the building up of spiritual power until one gained *moksha* (the final release from the cycle of birth and death). The sacred scriptures describe some of the super-human, almost god-like powers achieved by yogis. Some yogis are said to have used such powers for evil instead of good.

Over the centuries, a number of different schools of yoga have developed. In modern times, many people in India and in the West practise yoga without any religious aim. Supporters of yoga say it brings better health, improved powers of thinking, peace of mind and longer life.

## How it's done

The ancient writings set out a number of requirements for the yogi. These include self-control, non-violence, truthfulness, chastity and avoiding greed. There is a series of postures, called *asanas*, for training the body.

An important posture is the *padma asana* (lotus posture). Here the person sits with back erect and legs crossed so that the feet rest on the thighs. This posture is said to bring a peaceful mental state.

There are numerous other *asanas*. In the cobra posture you lie flat on the floor on your stomach, raising your head and shoulders. In the star posture you stand and bend at the waist so your forehead touches your knees.

**Left:** This picture of the goddess Parvati is made from a *mantra* (sacred word formula) which has been written over and over again.

**Above:** The syllable *'Om'* is often used as a mantra, either on its own or with other words.

**Left:** This is a yantra used for meditation. The circles, lotus petals and intersecting triangles help to focus concentration inwards.

## Yantras and Mantras

Hindus and Buddhists use similar aids to help concentration during meditation. Diagrams designed especially for this are called *yantras*. One example is shown on the left.

Verbal aids called *mantras* are also used. A guru may give each of his students his or her own mantra. The mantra is repeated over and over again. This is said to create vibrations which aid concentration and raise the spiritual level.

The syllable *'Om'* is frequently used in mantras. It may be repeated on its own or combined with other words. 'Om', written as it is on the left, is considered to be a symbol of spiritual good in Hinduism. Posters with the symbol 'Om' are found in many Hindu homes. Some people may paint it on the dashboard of their car, or wear it engraved on a pendant around the neck.

**Left:** A Hindu holy man or *sadhu*. Spiritual seekers like him use yoga to tap the powers of mind and body. This man holds prayer beads in his left hand. Next to him is a conch shell, which is sacred to the god Vishnu and used in some religious rites.

**Right:** A yoga class in Spain. Students are learning the *Padma Asana* or Lotus Posture.

Breathing exercises are also important. The yogi learns to control his breathing and to breathe in special rhythms. To build up powers of concentration, the yogi might use *yantras* (visual aids) or *mantras* (verbal aids). These are described in the box at the top of the page.

## Yoga spreads to the West

Books with descriptions of yogic exercises have sold millions of copies all over the world, and schools of yoga have been opened in almost every country. Most people in the West think of yoga as good exercise, but scientists are interested in finding out more about the subject. The holy men of Hinduism may one day provide the key for new ways of tapping the powers of the mind and body.

# Places of pilgrimage

## Pilgrimages as part of faith

For many Hindus, pilgrimages to religious centres or holy places are an important part of the faith. Hindus are not required to make such pilgrimages, but many people feel that a visit to a holy place brings religious merit.

It is not only the rich, who can travel in comfort, who make such journeys. Small groups of villagers often set out together in bullock carts, on trains and buses or on foot. The journey may be difficult, but it is also exciting. Often such visits are timed for special festivals held at pilgrimage spots. Most Indian villagers work seven days a week for most of the year. When the crops are harvested, a pilgrimage serves as a sort of holiday. Such trips are not expensive, because pilgrims are welcome in *dharmshalas* (temple guest houses), where they can stay free or pay a small donation.

**Right:** Foothills of the beautiful and awe-inspiring Himalayas. Their grandeur has made them one of Hinduism's holy places.

## Various sites

A Hindu pilgrim has many holy places to choose from. The great temples of Hinduism are high on the list. Many rivers and mountains are also considered sacred. There are many reasons why a spot might be considered holy. An important event may have happened there or the place may be mentioned in one of Hinduism's many myths. Or it may simply be a spot that is particularly beautiful or awe-inspiring.

## Bathing in the Ganges

The Ganges river is by far Hinduism's most important place of pilgrimage. The waters of the Ganges are said to wash away a person's sins, and most Hindus try to bathe in the river at least once in their lifetime.

One of the greatest religious centres on the shores of the Ganges is the city of Benares (sometimes known by its ancient name of Varanasi) where hundreds of temples line the river. One section along the water has been set aside as a cremation ground.

## Cremation

After death, Hindus cremate the body rather than bury it. The body is placed on a raised platform and covered with sandalwood. At the cremation ceremony, rituals are performed and hymns recited to remind mourners that the body perishes but the soul is immortal. Then the pyre is lit by the eldest son or another family member.

Many Hindus would like to die near the holy Ganges, or at least have their ashes scattered in the river. Relatives may carry the ashes from the distant corners of India, or the world, to the Ganges.

## Mountains and temples

The Himalayas, which are described as the abode of the gods in many stories, are another important pilgrimage spot. Each year hundreds of pilgrims make the difficult trek up Mount Kailasha in the central Himalayas, which is sacred to the god Shiva.

Among Hinduism's great temples, one of the most spectacular is the Jagannatha temple in the city of Puri. Hundreds of thousands of pilgrims gather here for a festival held in June or July. At this time an image of Jagannatha (a form of the god Vishnu) is taken in procession on a gigantic wooden vehicle (called a car). The car is about 14 metres high and has 16 wheels, each one over two metres in diameter. Pilgrims pull this through Puri's wide main street. The English word 'juggernaut' (which means a large vehicle) comes from the procession of Lord Jagannatha.

**Right:** A cremation ceremony. The body is covered with sandalwood and the pyre lit by the eldest son. Relatives will often make a pilgrimage to the river Ganges to scatter the ashes in its holy waters.

**Right:** Pilgrims at the Kumbha Mela gather to hear a holy man. The *Kumbha Mela* is celebrated once in six years at the place where the Ganges and Jamuna rivers meet, near the city of Allahabad. Over 2 million pilgrims gather for the event.

# A rich artistic heritage

**Right:** The marriage of Shiva and Parvati, in a wall painting from the Minakshi temple in Madurai. The scene was probably painted in the 17th century. Wall painting has a long history in India. Among the earliest surviving examples are the murals on the walls of the cave temples at Ajanta. Some of these date back to the first century BC.

## Hinduism, a source of ideas

An ancient Indian proverb says that the person who knows nothing of literature, music or art is nothing but a beast without the beast's tail and horns. In ancient India, art was an important part of life and the Hindu religion was one of the main inspirations of artists.

## Bringing stone to life

Stone sculpture dates back to at least 300BC in India. Hundreds of stone temples built across India prove the skill of a long line of artists. One of the main aims of the Indian sculptor was to bring life to the stone statues. A feeling of movement was created by the pose of the sculpted figure. Many Indian statues are carved in what is known as the *tri-bhanga* posture, in which the body follows three lines—the legs slanting at one angle, the trunk of the body at another and the head at a third angle. This pose makes the statues appear to have stopped in the midst of moving.

Indian sculptors wanted to show the very breath within a figure and used gently rounded curves to get the effect of the breath or life-force pushing outward. Unlike the Greeks, the Indians thought that the body should be shown with perfect smoothness rather than bulging muscles. The ornate jewellery on Indian statues contrasts with the even surface of the skin.

The gods and goddesses were a main subject of Indian artists, but these craftsmen also enjoyed carving ordinary people and

every sort of animal and plant. Many modern artists continue to use the techniques developed in ancient India. Others use new methods to interpret ancient themes.

## Music for the gods

Classical Indian music and dance were developed for performances held in the palace and the temple. Musical instruments have changed somewhat over the ages. Today among the most popular are the *sitar* (a stringed instrument), and the *tabla* (a small drum).

Classical Indian music is grouped into various tune types called *ragas*. There are six basic ragas. Each raga is suited to a particular time of day. The Megha raga, which is associated with peace and calm, should be played in the morning. The Kaushika raga, which is associated with joy and laughter, should be played at night.

## The art of dance

Many classical Indian dances tell religious stories. The dancer must have perfect control over his or her body because every movement and gesture is important. An ancient book on dance lists 36 movements for the eyes and 37 gestures for the hand, and numerous other postures and gestures for other parts of the body. The hand gestures, called *mudras*, are especially important in story telling. Classical music and dance are now performed mainly by trained professionals.

Art and craft remain an important part of life even in remote villages. Villagers paint beautiful patterns on the mud walls of their homes. Local craftsmen make clay and wooden figures for use in village shrines and homes.

**Right:** A gigantic statue of Shiva in a cave temple on the island of Elephanta in Bombay harbour. The statue probably dates back to the 8th century. This awe-inspiring work of art shows Shiva with three faces which represent the three sides of his nature. The face on the left is terrible and wrathful and that on the right is beautiful and peaceful. The face looking straight ahead is calm and aloof.

**Right:** Hinduism has inspired great painting and stone sculpture. Hindu myths are also the subject of much of India's fantastic folk art.

These tall male and female figures are being made for the holiday of Dussehra. They are covered with brightly coloured paper and will be stuffed with fire crackers. At the end of the 10-day celebrations, they will be burnt and go up in a shower of sparks and a cloud of smoke.

# Further information

## Useful words – a glossary

Every faith has special words used to describe its beliefs and practices. Some important terms for Hinduism are listed below. Many are from the Sanskrit language.

**ahimsa** non-violence; the belief in non-injury to people, animals and all living things.

**arti** a simple ceremony for showing reverence to a deity. An oil lamp is held in the hands and a circle of light made in front of an image of a god or goddess. Often performed at the beginning or end of a puja.

**asana** a set posture. Various asanas must be mastered in the practice of yoga.

**ascetic** a holy man. A person who practises self-denial as a means of religious discipline.

**ashram** a religious centre where priests and their followers live and work together. A Hindu might go to an ashram to study religion, seek spiritual guidance or simply to get away from the everyday world.

**ashramas** the stages of life. The four ashramas are that of *brahmacharin* (student), *grhastha* (householder), *vanaprasthya* (forest dweller) and *sanyasin* (wandering holy man).

**Atman** the self, the soul.

**avatar** an incarnation on earth of a god, especially the god Vishnu. Rama and Krishna are Vishnu's most widely worshipped avatars.

**bhakti** devotion, especially loving devotion to a personal god.

**bindi** a red dot or other decorative mark worn on the forehead by many Hindu women. A bindi has no special religious significance.

**Brahman** the World Spirit or World Soul. The essence that pervades the universe and is also the individual soul.

**Brahmin** (also sometimes spelt Brahman) the priestly class. The highest of the four classes or *varnas*.

**caste** the division of Hindu society into groups which are ranked one above the other. Caste is determined by birth and is often based on an occupation which is handed down from father to son. Most caste groups do not marry with members of other castes.

**cremation** the usual Hindu funeral practice, in which the dead body is reduced to ashes by fire.

**dharma** sacred law, the rules by which one should conduct one's life, also one's duties in life.

**dharmshala** a rest house for pilgrims usually built near a temple.

**four ends of life** in religious texts, three main aims are assigned to the householder stage of life: *dharma* (gaining merit by following the sacred law); *artha* (gaining wealth in honest ways); and *kama* (the enjoyment of the pleasures of life). The fourth end, *moksha* (release), is to be sought in the third and fourth stages of life.

**ghee** clarified butter. Used in many Hindu ceremonies.

**guru** teacher, especially a Brahmin who acts as a spiritual guide.

**Harijan** a name Gandhi gave the untouchables. It means 'Children of God'.

**horoscope** a diagram showing the position of the planets and the signs of the zodiac at the time a person was born. Used by astrologers in an effort to foretell events in a person's life.

**jati** caste group. Hundreds of jati make up the caste system.

**karma** the effect of past deeds. The influence of past deeds in determining one's status in this life and the next.

**Kshatriya** the warrior class; the second highest of the four classes or *varnas*.

**mantra** a verse or phrase believed to have religious or magical powers.

**moksha** liberation, release, salvation, enlightenment.

**mudra** hand gestures with set meanings used in dance, drama and religion.

**Om** a very sacred and auspicious syllable. A symbol for the whole of creation.

**puja** the main Hindu form of worship. Often in an Indian household a simple, everyday ceremony in which prayers are offered and flowers and food are placed before a deity.

**rishi** sage, wise man.

**sacred thread** a loop of thread given to boys of the upper three classes at the time of an initiation ceremony, and worn over the left shoulder and under the right arm from that time onward.

**sadhu** a holy man, an ascetic.

**samsara** the cycle of birth and death.

**sanyasin** a wandering holy man. One who has renounced the world.

**shakti** power, usually female energy

represented by the goddess.

**shanti** the Sanskrit word for 'peace'.

**shraddha** rites performed in commemoration of ancestors.

**Shudra** the lowest of the four classes or varnas. Members traditionally do manual labour or serve the higher classes in other ways.

**tilak** a mark on the forehead usually made with red powder and applied during a puja.

**twice born** those who have undergone the sacred thread ceremony, which is said to be a second birth.

**Untouchable** a person who is outside the four classes or varnas and was traditionally considered impure. Untouchables did, and often still do, the most unpleasant jobs, such as cleaning streets and lavatories.

**Vaishya** the third class or varna, usually concerned with trade or business.

**varnas** the four classes of Hindu society: *Brahmins* (priests), *Kshatriyas* (warriors), *Vaishyas* (traders and businessmen), *Shudras* (manual workers).

**varnashrama dharma** the right code (*dharma*) for leading one's life, based on the *varna* (or class) one was born into and the *ashrama* (or stage of life) that one is at.

**yantra** a mystical diagram that may be used as an aid to meditation.

**yoga** a system of exercises and meditation aimed at gaining control of mind and body.

**yugas** four long eras that make up the Hindu cycle of time. The names of the yugas are Kryta, Treta, Dvapara and Kali. In the Kryta yuga things are at their best and people are happy. In each of the following yugas, things get progressively worse. We are currently in the worst of all yugas, the Kali yuga, which still has thousands of years to run.

# Special dates

Hinduism has many holidays. Several festivals are discussed on pages 30 and 31. Here are twelve other important dates on the festival calendar:

**Lohri** (January) Celebrated mainly in the North Indian state of Punjab to mark the end of the winter season. Bonfires are lit as part of the celebrations.

**Pongal-Sankranti** (January–February) A three-day festival celebrated in South India at the time of the rice harvest.

**Vasant Panchmi** (January–February) A spring festival during which Saraswati, goddess of wisdom and learning, is especially worshipped. An important holiday for students.

**Ramakrishna Utsava** (February 20) The birthday of the 19th-century saint, Ramakrishna. Celebrated especially in his home-state of Bengal. Centres of the Ramakrishna Mission in Europe and the USA hold special programmes.

**Shivaratri** (February–March) The main festival honouring the god Shiva, celebrated throughout India. Worshippers fast for the day and night of Shivaratri and keep an all-night vigil at Shiva temples, where hymns are sung, prayers offered and the Shiva stories told.

**Baisakhi** (April–May) Celebrated especially in the Punjab at the time of the winter harvest. A dance called the Bhangra is performed, in which villagers act out the sowing and harvesting of the crop.

**Teej** (June–July) A festival for women and girls honouring the goddess Parvati, wife of Shiva. Swings are hung from trees and in courtyards. Girls dress up in their best clothes, swing and sing hymns to Parvati.

**Raksha Bandhan** (July–August) A special holiday for brothers and sisters. Girls tie a piece of thread or ribbon called a *rakhi* round the right wrist of each brother to wish them good fortune and protection from evil. In return, brothers give their sisters presents and promise to protect them.

**Janmashtami** (August–September) Celebration of the birthday of Lord Krishna. Worshippers fast for the day. When the moon is visible, a special puja is performed and the fast broken. Songs in praise of Krishna are sung and stories told.

**Onam** (August–September) Celebrated mainly in the South Indian state of Kerala to mark the end of the summer monsoon. Beautiful floral decorations are made and boat races held as part of the festivities.

**Ganesh Chaturthi** (August–September) The main festival honouring Lord Ganesh. Celebrated with great enthusiasm in Bombay, where large images of Ganesh are carried in a spectacular procession.

**Gandhi Jayanti** (October 2) Mahatma Gandhi's birthday, which is celebrated as a national holiday in India. Gandhi combined the roles of politician and religious leader.

# Books for further reading

*Religions of India* by Thomas Berry (Glencoe)

*The Sacred Thread* by J.L. Brockington (Columbia University Press, 1981)

*Hinduism* by Yorke Crompton (International Publication Service, 1976)

*Guide to the Hindu Religion* by David J. Dell (G.K. Hall, 1981)

*Hinduism* by I.G. Edmunds (Franklin Watts, 1979)

*Everyday Life in Early India* by Michael Edwardes (Putnam, 1969)

*Many People, Many Faiths: An Introduction to the Religious Life of Mankind* by Robert Ellwood Jr. (Prentice-Hall, 1976)

*The Hindu Tradition* by Ainslee T. Embree (Random House, 1972)

*India Now and Through Time* by Catherine A. Galbraith and Rama Mehta (Houghton Mifflin, 1980)

*The Hindu Religious Tradition* by Thomas Hopkins (Dickenson, 1971)

*God and Gods in Hinduism* by Donald Johnson and Jean Johnson (Humanities Press, 1972)

*Learning About People and Cultures: India* (McDougal-Littell)

*The Hindu Temple* by George Michell (Harper and Row, 1978)

*Hindu Gods and Godesses* by A.G. Mitchell and John Lowry (State Mutual Books, 1982)

*Hindu Myths* by Wendy O'Flaherty (Penguin Books, 1975)

*Hinduism: Religion and a Way of Life* by Satyavrata Patel (Asia Book Corp., 1980)

*Bhagavad-Gita: Song of God* by Swami Prabhavananda, translated by Christopher Ishewood (Vedanta Press)

*Upanishads* by Swami Prabhavananda, translated by Frederick Manchester (Vedanta Press)

*The Hindu View of Life* by S. Radhakrishan (Allen Unwin, 1980)

*Bullock Carts and Motor Bikes: Ancient India on a New Road* by Beth Roy (Atheneum, 1972)

*Srimad Ramayana: The Prince of Ayodhya* by D.S. Sarma (Vedanta Press)

*Hinduism* by Kshitimohan M. Sen (Penguin Books, 1962)

*Festivals of India* by B.N. Sharma (South Asia Books)

*A Hindu Boyhood* by Sharat Shetty (M. Evans, 1970)

*Historic India* by Lucille Shulberg (Time-Life Books, 1968)

*Great Religions of the World* by Huston Smith, et. al. (National Geographic Society, 1978)

*India* by Natasha Talyarkhan (Silver Burdett, 1977)

*Hindu Religion, Customs, and Manners* by P. Thomas (Apt Books, 1981)

*India: The Challenge of Change* by James Traub (Julian Messner, 1981)

*Hinduism* by Robert C. Zaehner (Oxford University Press, 1962)

# Places to visit

A visit to a Hindu temple is one of the best ways to learn about Hinduism.

Hindu friends or neighbors will be able to tell you the location of the Hindu temple nearest to your home or school. Most temples are happy to welcome groups of students who are learning about Hinduism, but arrangements should be made in advance by making personal contact with a priest or committee member.

# Helpful organizations

These organizations can all offer help and useful information. Don't forget to enclose a stamped, self-addressed envelope when you write.

**The Friends of India Society International**
P.O. Box 4922
Falls Church, Virginia   22044

**The Indian Embassy**
2107 Massachusetts Avenue, NW
Washington, DC   20008

# Index

Agni 14, 15
Alexander the Great 11
America (also see USA) 37
Arjuna 28, 29, 34
Arranged marriages 20, 21, 22, 26
Art 10, 11, 12, 13, 40, 41
Arti 23, 42
Aryabhata 11
Aryans 10, 11
Asana 36, 37, 42
Ashoka 11
Ashramas 19, 42
Atman 10, 17, 34, 35, 42
Avatars 13, 28, 30, 34, 42

Bali 9
Barber 21
Basic beliefs 16, 17, 18, 19
Basketmakers 20
Benares (also see Varanasi) 8, 38
Bhagavad Gita 34
Bhakti (also see devotion) 10, 42
Bhave, Vinobha 11
Birth of a baby 24
Brahma (god) 13, 14, 15
Brahman (World Soul) 10, 12, 14, 16, 17, 34, 42
Brahmin (priestly caste) 18, 24, 25, 26, 42
Bride 22, 26, 27
Britain (also see England) 9, 10, 11, 32, 33
Buddhism 9, 10, 11, 37

Calendar 30
Canada 9
Caste 18, 19, 20, 21, 42
Ceremonies: birth 24, naming 24, sacred thread 24, 25, marriage 26, 27, funeral 38, 39
Chandra 14, 15
Childhood 24, 25
Chola dynasty 11
Christianity 10, 11, 12, 32
Conch shell 13, 14, 36, 37
Cow 29
Cremation 38, 39, 42
Cycle of birth and death 12, 16, 17, 34, 36

Dance 12, 25, 29, 40
Devi 14
Devotion (also see bhakti) 10, 17, 34
Dharma 9, 19, 42
Dharmshala 38, 42
Divali 30
Durga 14, 15, 30, 31
Dussehra 25, 30, 41

England (also see Britain) 9, 23, 25, 26

Europe 9, 10, 37

Family life 22, 23, 24, 25
Family priest 24
Family shrine 22, 23, 30
Festivals 30, 31, 38, 41, 43
Fire 14, 24, 26, 27
Folk art 41

Gandhi, Mahatma 11, 20
Ganesh 14
Ganges River cover, 8, 10, 16–17, 38, 39
Ghee 24, 26, 42
Gods and goddesses 8, 10, 12, 13, 14, 15, 22, 28, 29, 30, 31, 32, 40
Groom 26, 27
Gupta empire 11
Guru 9, 37, 42

Hanuman 14, 15, 30
Harijans 20, 42
Himalayas 38
History of Hinduism 10
Holi 30
Holidays 25, 30, 31, 43
Holy books (see sacred books)
Holy men 13, 19, 36, 37, 39
Holy places 38, 39
Horoscope 24, 42
Hymns and songs 10, 11, 25, 34

Incarnation (see avatar)
Indra 14
Indus valley 10, 11
Islam 9, 10, 11

Jainism 10, 11
Jati 18, 42

Kali 14, 15
Karma 16, 18, 19, 42
Krishna 13, 22, 28, 29, 34
Kshatriya 18, 25, 42
Kumbha Mela 39

Lakshmi 13, 14, 30
Laws of Manu 11
Linga 32, 33
Lotus posture 36, 37

Mahabharata 11, 28, 29, 34
Mahavira 10, 11
Mantras 37, 42
Marriage 20, 21, 22, 26, 27
Meditation 17, 19, 22, 37
Mirabai 11
Moksha 17, 34, 36, 42
Mother goddess 10
Mudra 40, 42
Music 40
Muslims 9, 10, 11, 12, 32

Naming ceremony 24, 25
Nanak, Guru 11, 25
Nandi 32, 33
Navratri 25
Nepal 8

Om 37, 42
Origin of the word 'Hindu' 9

Padma asana 36, 37
Painting 13, 40
Pakistan 11
Pallava dynasty 11
Parvati 14, 37, 40
Paths to salvation 17
Pilgrimage 8, 38, 39
Potter 21
Prayer (also see puja, worship) 19, 22, 23
Prayer beads 13, 22, 36, 37
Priest 24, 25, 26, 27, 32, 33, 34
Puja 9, 14, 22, 23, 31, 32, 42
Puranas 34

Radhakrishnan, S. 11
Raga 40
Rama 12, 13, 14, 22, 25, 30, 34
Ramakrishna 11
Rama Lila 30
Ramanuja 11
Ramayana 11, 30, 34
Ravana 30, 34
Rebirth (also see cycle of birth and death) 18, 19
Respect for elders 22
Rich and poor 18, 19
Rig Veda 10, 11, 34
Rites of passage (also see ceremonies) 24
Ritual purity 20

Sacred books 9, 10, 25, 26, 34, 35
Sacred law 9, 19
Sacred thread 24, 25, 42
Sacrifice 10
Sadhu 36, 37, 42
Sanskrit 25, 26, 30, 34, 35
Sanyasi 19, 42
Saraswati 14, 15
Sari 22, 26, 27
Science 11
Sculpture 10, 11, 40
Sects 13
Serpents and snakes 10, 11, 13, 28, 29
Shakti 14, 42
Shankara 11
Shesha 13
Shiva 10, 12, 13, 32, 34, 38, 40
Shudra 18, 43
Sikhism 9, 10, 11, 25
Sita 14, 25, 30, 34

Sitar 40
South-East Asia 10, 11
Spain 37
Spread of Hinduism 9, 10, 11
Stages of life 19, 24
Statues 12, 13, 22, 23, 32, 40
Stick dance 25
Surya 14, 15
Symbols in Hindu art 12, 13

Tabla 40
Teachers (also see guru) 9, 10, 25, 37
Temples and shrines 8, 9, 14, 22, 23, 32, 33, 34, 38, 40
Tilak 31, 43
Time 12, 13, 43
Trinidad 9
Twice born 25, 43

Untouchables 18, 20, 43
Upanishads 10, 11, 34, 35
USA 9

Vaishya 18, 25, 43
Varanasi (also see Benares) cover, 38
Varnas 18, 43
Vedas (also see Rig Veda) 14, 34
Villages 8, 9, 20, 21, 22, 38
Vishnu 10, 12, 13, 14, 24, 28, 30, 34, 37, 38

Wedding (see marriage)
West Indies 9
Women 8, 9, 22, 23, 26, 27
World Soul 10, 12, 14, 16, 17, 34
Worship (also see puja) 8, 9, 31, 32, 33, 34

Yantras 37, 43
Yoga 17, 22, 36, 37, 43

## Illustration credits

Key to position of illustrations:
(T) top, (C) centre, (B) bottom, (R) right, (L) left.

### Artists

Nick Farmer: 8
Nanda Kumara: 35
Tony Payne: 28–29, 32–33, 37
Shyam Varma: 13, 14–15

### Photographic sources

Patricia Bahree: 37(TL), 38 (courtesy Victoria and Albert Museum)
Cam Culbert: 19(T)
Daily Telegraph Colour Library: endpapers, 19(B)
Douglas Dickens: cover, 34, 40(T)
Halcyon/L. Baker: 16–17
Robert Harding Picture Library/Sassoon: 30
Michael Holford: 11, 12, 13, 40(B)
John & Penny Hubley: title page, 24(T)
Alan Hutchison Library: 22, 27(T), 36, 41
Robert Jackson: 23(B), 25(T)
Bury Peerless: 8, 9, 20, 21, 23(T), 27(B), 29, 31, 39(T), contents page
Jan Siegieda: 26
H. Daniel Smith/Syracuse University, New York: 24(B)
ZEFA: 37(BR), 39(B)

5 6 7 8 9 10—U—90 89 88 87 86